The Sock Knitting Kit

Six Splendid Patterns for Toasty Toes

BY ALYCE BENEVIDES &
JAQUELINE MILLES

CHRONICLE BOOKS
SAN FRANCISCO

ISBN: 978-0-8118-6592-0

Manufactured in China

Design by Lesley Feldman

Chronicle Books endeavors
to use environmentally
responsible paper in its gift
and stationery products.

10 9 8 7 6 5 4 3 2 1

Chronicle Books LLC
680 Second Street
San Francisco, CA 94107

www.chroniclebooks.com

Table of Contents

Introduction

There are many kinds of knitters: patient, careful ones who plan out intricate and time-consuming projects; those who have several projects going on at once; those who can't quite seem to finish anything they start; and those who seek instant gratification and are entirely too impatient for long-term projects. A pair of socks is a perfect project for all of these knitters. Socks can be knit quickly enough to please the impatient, and they are lovely little side projects if you want to get away from that big, looming task. Knitting an accessory that doesn't take weeks to complete is always satisfying. Their small size allows you to indulge in a luxurious yarn, such as cashmere, and being able to knit them speedily makes them great spontaneous gifts.

Socks are a bit daunting if you've never tried knitting them before. If you take some time to deconstruct the parts of the sock, however, you will demystify the whole process and be well on your way to making one, or even a pair!

Basically, a sock is just a tube that is closed on one end. Sure, you could knit just that and have a rather ill fitting thing. With a little tweaking, though, you can make a perfectly fitted, customized little treat. The six patterns provided in this kit are for specific sizes and gauges, but after just one or two attempts you should be able to customize the instructions based on a few measurements of the intended wearer's foot and leg.

First and foremost, you must knit in the round to form a tube, usually knitting the sock from the cuff down. We prefer using five double-pointed needles, where up to four needles hold the tube and the fifth needle is used to work the round. When you join the round, place a marker or leave the tail of yarn from your cast-on row hanging. The marker at the beginning of the round will indicate the back center of your sock. The first needle's stitches you knit (which we'll call Needle 1) will be half of the back, then the next two needles' stitches (Needles 2 and 3) will become the front part of the sock.

And then, with the five little adjustments described below you can transform your basic tube into a fitted garment:

01 Knit the Heel Flap

To start the heel, place all of the instep stitches from Needles 2 and 3 on a holder. The combined stitches from Needles 1 and 4 are now worked in rows (not rounds) to create the flap. A heel is generally knit in as many rows as there are stitches on Needles 1 and 4, which is half of your total stitches. So if you cast on 40 stitches, use 20 stitches to create a heel, and knit these 20 stitches for 20 rows. When working these 20 rows, slip the first stitch of each row to form a neat selvage.

02 Turn the Heel

After the square flap of the heel is completed, continue knitting in rows on the heel stitches to turn the heel. This will make the short rows and decreases that begin to give the sock its L-shape. Once the heel is turned, go back to working in rounds.

03 Form the Gussets

For your sock to have that L-shape from ankle to foot, gussets must be formed. By picking up stitches on the selvages and eventually working decreases on both sides of the heel, you can form a triangular gusset. Start with working the instep stitches on the holders back into the round, and pick up stitches along the selvages of the heel flap. This is where the slipped stitches on your heel flap play an important role. Because you slipped the first stitch, your selvage should be about half of the number of rows you knitted, plus 1 for the turned heel. So in our example where we had 20 heel stitches and 20 rows of flap, we would then pick up 11 (half plus 1) stitches along each selvage. Then a series of decreases on each side of the heel complete the L-shape and bring you back to your original number of desired stitches. At this point, simply continue working in rounds for several inches to make the instep—the part of the tube that covers the foot—until you reach the base of the toe.

04 Shape the Toe

For simple toe shaping, a basic pattern of mirrored decreases is worked in four places along the sock. You will be decreasing on the top left and right, while working the symmetrical mirrored decreases on the bottom left and right of the sock, until you have only 8 to 10 stitches left.

05 Finish the Sock

You can use a Kitchener stitch or any other bind off method of your choice to close the sock tube. When we started making socks, the Kitchener stitch (also known as grafting) was the most difficult part to master. It's hard to believe we would get through an entire sock of beautiful ornate work, then be frustrated by those pesky last few stitches! But it's well worth the practice to master this stitch. It seams without any bumps or lumps, and gives your project a neat, accomplished-looking finish.

If you're reading over the instructions and are still hesitant about the intricacies of "knit 2 together" or "slip, slip, knit" or what it really is to "pick up stitches" anyway, just relax! "Knit 2 together" and "slip, slip, knit" are both ways of taking two stitches and making them into one: just a simple decrease. If this seems complicated to you at first, just knit 2 together whenever a decrease is called for. All that will happen is that the symmetry of your knitting will be a bit unfinished. It's a great idea to try this for a first practice sock, however. You will begin to visualize what all the instructions mean. Similarly, picking up stitches seems confusing at first: You may not be sure if something is the selvage, or just the yarn between two stitches. It may not be as easy to spot or as neat as you'd like. Or should you use four double-pointed needles or five? Do not fret. Just make a practice sock and fudge it as best you can. We guarantee that, with a bit of practice, it will all click!

* The Projects *

Cheerleader Socks!

~ Classic Ped Socks with Pom-poms ~

We wore socks like these as kids in the 1970s. Not only are they cute, they're a perfect project for beginners. We jazzed these up with simple intarsia hearts on the heel flaps and pink toes, but you can knit them in a solid color if you prefer. Using size 4 needles, we produced a very tight knit and thicker fabric reminiscent of terry cloth. The pink accent was done with two strands of lightweight/sport yarn, simply because we couldn't find the perfect pink in worsted-weight. If you find a complementary color in the same type yarn as you use for the white sock, feel free to use that. Remember, do not double it if you use the heavier yarn.

We recommend this as a sock for beginners, great to try out with any worsted-weight yarn you may have in your stash. These nostalgic anklets may have you searching for your white canvas sneakers!

Materials

* 5 double-pointed needles
  (size 4, or size required
  to obtain correct gauge)
* Stitch marker
* Stitch holder
* Thin cardboard
* Darning needle
* 2 skeins white worsted-weight
  extra-fine merino yarn (we used 115
  yards of Karabella Yarns, Aurora 8,
  #1250, for the pair)
* 1 skein pink lightweight/sport
  extra-fine merino yarn (we used 100
  yards of Karabella Yarns, Aurora 4,
  #9, for the pair, including pom-poms)

Gauge (in stockinette stitch)

* 6 stitches per inch

Finished Size

* ladies' medium/large

Skills & Methods

* Stockinette stitch
* Intarsia
* Kitchener stitch

ᘒᕉ Cast On & Knit the Ankle ᕉᘒ

Using the double cast-on method, cast on 40 stitches in doubled pink yarn onto 1 needle. Next, divide the stitches evenly onto 4 needles, 10 stitches on each needle. Join the round, being careful not to twist the stitches. Place a stitch marker at the beginning of the round, between Needles 1 and 4.

To create the ribbed edge, repeat knit 1, purl 1 for 3 rows. Change to white yarn, and work 4 rows in stockinette stitch.

ᘔ⤳ Knit the Heel Flap ⤳ᘔ

Transfer the stitches on Needles 2 and 3 onto a stitch holder. We will not be knitting the instep or knitting rounds while we work on the heel flap. We will instead be constructing the heel flap from the 20 stitches on Needles 1 and 4. Work 10 stitches in stockinette stitch to the end of Needle 1 with Needle 2. Turn your work, slip 1, and purl 19 stitches.

Keep working the heel flap in stockinette stitch for a total of 20 rows, making sure to slip the first stitch of each knit and purl row. This will create a selvage seam of 11 loops for the gusset later. If you would like to include the heart design on the heel, work 3 rows in stockinette stitch and then follow the intarsia graph, on page 18, starting at the top of the heart (row 1 on the graph), since you are knitting from the top down.

ᘔ⤳ Turn the Heel ⤳ᘔ

Still working with your 20 stitches, do the following:

* **row 1:** Knit to 2 beyond center (in other words, 12 stitches), slip slip knit, knit 1, turn.

* **row 2:** Slip 1, purl 5, purl 2 together, purl 1, turn.

* **row 3:** Slip 1, knit to 1 stitch before the gap from the prior row, slip slip knit, knit 1, turn.

* **row 4:** Slip 1, purl to 1 stitch before the gap from the prior row, purl 2 together, purl 1, turn.

Continue repeating rows 3 and 4 until only 12 stitches remain. On your last set of rows, you will have to skip the last knit 1 or purl 1 since no more stitches will be left.

2✦ Form the Gussets ✦2

We now return to working in the round. To give your sock that L-shape from ankle to foot you will need to pick up stitches on the selvages, and work the instep stitches on the holders back into the round. When you pick up stitches along the selvage, feel free to use your preferred method. We chose to pick up through both halves of the edge stitch, and to loop through from the right side to the wrong side, leaving a raised edge to decorate the outside of the sock. To do this, work as follows:

* **needle 1:** Knit across all 12 heel stitches, then pick up 11 stitches along the selvage.

* **needle 2:** Work across 10 stitches on the holder.

* **needle 3:** Work across the remaining 10 stitches on the holder.

* **needle 4:** Pick up 11 stitches along the selvage, and knit 6 from Needle 1.

You should now have 54 stitches total: 17 stitches on Needle 1, 10 stitches on Needle 2, 10 stitches on Needle 3, and 17 stitches on Needle 4.

To decrease along Needles 1 and 4 and get your sock's width back to 40 stitches, work decrease rounds every other round as follows:

* **needle 1:** Knit to last 3 stitches, knit 2 together, knit 1.

* **needle 2:** Knit across.

* **needle 3:** Knit across.

* **needle 4:** Knit 1, slip slip knit, knit to end.

Remember to work a round without decreases in between each decreasing round. Repeat this pattern until only 10 stitches remain on each needle.

16

❧ Knit the Instep ❧

Knit even until the sock measures 7 inches from the back of the heel, or is the desired length to the base of the toes (in our case, 40 rows).

❧ Shape the Toe ❧

If you like, switch to the doubled pink yarn, or else continue with white yarn. Knit 4 rounds. To begin basic toe shaping, decrease 4 stitches every other round as follows:

* **needle 1:** Knit to 3 stitches from the end, knit 2 together, knit 1.

* **needle 2:** Knit 1, slip slip knit, knit to end.

* **needle 3:** Knit to 3 stitches from the end, knit 2 together, knit 1.

* **needle 4:** Knit 1, slip slip knit, knit to end.

Once you have a total of 20 stitches remaining (5 stitches on each needle), work the above decreases every round until only 2 stitches remain on each needle. Combine the stitches on Needles 1 and 4 onto 1 needle, and the stitches on Needles 2 and 3 onto another needle. Create a seam using the Kitchener stitch or the 3-needle bind off. Turn the sock inside out and weave in the loose threads, with the exception of your dangling cast-on yarn.

❧ Make Pom-poms ❧

Cut out 2 cardboard circles, each 1 inch in diameter. Cut out a smaller circle from the center of each. Hold the 2 doughnut-shaped rings together. Cut the pink yarn into manageable lengths (about 3–4 yards) and wrap the yarn around the rings until they are completely covered and the center hole is nearly full. (The more yarn you use, the fuller the finished pompom will be.) Insert the tip of a pair of scissors between the circles, and cut the yarn all along the perimeter. Tie a piece of yarn very tightly in between the circles, then remove the cardboard. Voilà! You have a pom-pom! Trim and repeat. Sew a pompom to the back of each sock using the dangling yarn from the cast-on.

⌁ Heart Graph ⌁

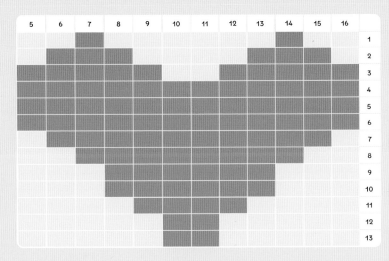

The Sock Knitting Kit

Unisex Socks

⌁ Ribbed Mid-Calf Socks ⌁

Once you master this basic sock pattern, we hope you are inspired to begin designing your own socks. This simple shape can be worn by a man or a woman and can be used as the basis for a myriad of versions, limited only by your imagination. By simply changing the yarn, the ribbing pattern, or the stitch, you can create socks that are all your own design. The yarn and needles included in this kit work for these socks, so let's begin!

Materials

* 5 double-pointed needles
  (size 3, or size required
  to obtain correct gauge)
* Stitch marker
* Stitch holder
* Darning needle
* 2 skeins Turquoise sport weight 100%
  alpaca yarn (we used 260 yards of
  Blue Sky Alpacas, #532, for the pair)

Gauge (in stockinette stitch)

* 6 stitches per inch in worsted-
  weight, 7 stitches per inch in
  sport weight

Skills & Methods

* Stockinette stitch
* Ribbing
* Kitchener stitch

Finished Size

* ladies' medium/large, or men's
  small/medium (worsted)
  ladies' small/medium (sport)

⇒ Cast On & Knit the Leg ⇐

Using the double cast-on method, cast on 52 stitches with the Turquoise yarn onto 1 needle. Divide the stitches evenly onto 4 needles, 13 stitches on each needle. Join the round, being careful not to twist the stitches. Place a stitch marker at the beginning of the round, between Needles 1 and 4.

We chose to do this entire sock in a knit 2, purl 2 rib, but feel free to do it in the rib or stitch of your choice. To create the rib we chose, alternately knit 2 stitches then purl 2 stitches for 6 rounds. Work in stockinette stitch until the leg measures approximately 8 inches (about 64 rounds).

Knit the Heel Flap

To knit the heel flap, divide your stitches as follows: knit 13 stitches to the end of Needle 1. Transfer the 26 stitches from Needles 2 and 3 onto a stitch holder. (You will work these stitches later when you create the instep.) Transfer your 13 stitches from Needle 4 onto the end of Needle 1. At this stage you will stop knitting rounds while you work on the heel flap, which is created from the 26 stitches now on Needle 1. Turn your work, slip 1, and purl back 25 stitches on Needle 1. To make the heel stronger than a stockinette-knitted fabric, we recommend knitting the heel flap in a heel stitch, which is done by slipping every other stitch on each purl row. Work 26 rows in heel stitch, making sure you slip the first stitch of each knit and purl row. This will create a selvage seam of 13 on each side of the heel flap for the gusset.

Turn the Heel

For a square heel, still working with your 26 stitches on Needle 1, do the following:

* **row 1:** Knit to 2 beyond center (in other words, 15 stitches), slip slip knit, knit 1, turn.

* **row 2:** Slip 1, purl 5, purl 2 together, purl 1, turn.

* **row 3:** Slip 1, knit to 1 stitch before the gap from the prior row, slip slip knit, knit 1, turn.

* **row 4:** Slip 1, purl to 1 stitch before the gap from the prior row, purl 2 together, purl 1, turn.

Repeat rows 3 and 4 until 14 stitches remain. On your last set of rows, you will have to skip the last knit 1 or purl 1 since no more stitches will be left.

⌁ Form the Gussets ⌁

You are now ready to connect the heel to the instep by picking up stitches along the selvages and returning to working in the round. Remember to continue the knit 2, purl 2 rib stitch when working the stitches on Needles 2 and 3. Begin by knitting across all 14 stitches on Needle 1. Next, pick up 1 stitch through each slip stitch loop along the edge of the heel flap, 14 stitches in total. You should now have 28 stitches on Needle 1. Transfer the 26 stitches from the stitch holder equally onto Needles 2 and 3, and work the rib pattern across. With Needle 4, pick up 1 stitch through each selvage on the other side of the heel flap, 14 stitches total, and knit the first 7 stitches of Needle 1. You should now have 68 stitches in total: 21 stitches each on Needles 1 and 4, and 13 stitches each on Needles 2 and 3.

Decrease for the gussets every other round as follows:

* **needle 1:** Knit to the last 3 stitches, knit 2 together, knit 1.

* **needle 2:** Work the rib pattern across.

* **needle 3:** Work the rib pattern across.

* **needle 4:** Knit 1, slip slip knit, knit to the end.

Repeat this decrease round for approximately 16 rounds, until 52 stitches remain, remembering to work a round without decreases in between each decrease round. Divide the stitches evenly among the 4 needles, 13 stitches per needle.

Knit the Instep

Knit even until the sock measures 8 inches from the back of the heel, or is the desired length to the base of the toes (approximately 50 rounds). Remember to work the stitches on Needles 2 and 3 in the knit 2, purl 2 rib.

Shape the Toe

Switch to stockinette stitch, decreasing 4 stitches every other round as follows to create the basic toe shaping:

* **needle 1:** Knit to 3 stitches from the end, knit 2 together, knit 1.

* **needle 2:** Knit 1, slip slip knit, knit to end.

* **needle 3:** Knit to 3 stitches from the end, knit 2 together, knit 1.

* **needle 4:** Knit 1, slip slip knit, knit to end.

Alternate this decrease round with 1 knit round until 28 stitches remain (approximately 11 rounds). Now that you have 7 stitches on each needle, work the above decreases every round until only 2 stitches remain on each needle. Transfer the remaining 8 stitches to 2 needles by combining the stitches on Needles 1 and 4, then combining those on Needles 2 and 3. Close the toe using the Kitchener stitch, and weave in the loose threads.

Toddlers
Bobby
Socks

～ Simple Lace and Ribbing Ankle Socks ～

Knitting gifts for friends and family is great fun, and knitting for children is particularly special. It will bring a smile to your face every time you see these socks worn. We were inspired by the classic images of little girls in pinafore dresses and patent leather Mary Janes when we designed this frilled bobby sock. The lace pattern is so simple that even a novice knitter shouldn't shy away. If you want to skip the lace work altogether, or amend the instructions to make a boy's version, that's easy too.

Materials

* 5 double-pointed needles
  (size 2, or size required
  to obtain correct gauge)
* Stitch marker
* Stitch holder
* Darning needle

* 2 skeins lavender lightweight/sport
  extra-fine merino yarn (we used 158
  yards of Karabella Yarns, Aurora 4,
  #12, for the pair) for the cuffed version
  or
* 2 skeins gray lightweight/sport extra-
  fine merino yarn (we used 158 yards
  of Koigu Painter's Palette Premium
  Merino Multi, #312 for the pair) for the
  plain version

Gauge (in stockinette stitch)

* 6.5 stitches per inch

Finished Size

* toddler, 18 months to 2 years old

Skills & Methods

* Stockinette stitch
* Basic rib stitch
* Kitchener stitch

❧ Cast On & Knit the Leg ❧

For the frilly, cuffed version:

Because we are going to be repeating a pattern on the instep of the sock eventually, we suggest using only 4 needles to knit up this sock. Using the double
cast-on method, cast on 120 stitches in lavender yarn onto 1 needle. Divide the
stitches evenly onto 3 needles, 40 stitches on each needle. Join the round, being
careful not to twist the stitches. Place a stitch marker at the beginning of the
round, between Needles 1 and 3, or just use your dangling yarn from your cast
on as an indicator of the beginning of the round.

To create the frilly edge, purl your first row. After this row, work in stockinette stitch by knitting every round. On the second round, knit 2 together throughout so that you have only 20 stitches left on each needle (a total of 60 stitches). On the third round, continue decreasing with a knit 2 together followed by a knit 1 pattern throughout the round. You will end up with the desired total of 40 stitches. The 3 needles holding your work, then, should be Needle 1, which holds the 10 stitches on the right side of heel; Needle 2, which holds all 20 of the instep stitches; and Needle 3, which holds the remaining 10 stitches of the heel side of the sock. Now you will introduce the following lace pattern every 3 rounds. It is a simple knit 2 together, yarn over pattern that repeats every 5 stitches to create 8 eyelets across the round. Every 3 rounds, the knit 2 together, yarn over is placed 1 stitch over from the preceding eyelet row in order to create the spiraling effect. The pattern is as follows:

⌒ Simple Eyelet Spirals ⌒

* **round 1:** From the beginning marker, *knit 2 together, yarn over, knit 3, repeat from the * throughout the round.

* **rounds 2–3:** Knit, work even.

* **round 4:** From the beginning marker, knit 1 then *knit 2 together, yarn over, knit 3, repeat from the *, but on your last eyelet, knit 2 together, yarn over, and finally knit 2 to end the round.

* **rounds 5–6:** Knit, work even.

* **round 7:** From the beginning marker, knit 2 then *knit 2 together, yarn over, knit 3, repeat from the *, but on your last eyelet, knit 2 together, yarn over, and finally knit 1 to end round.

* **rounds 8–9:** Knit, work even.

* **round 10:** From the beginning marker, knit 3 then *knit 2 together, yarn over, knit 3, repeat from the *, but on your last eyelet, knit 2 together and end the round with your yarn over.

* **rounds 11–12:** Knit, work even.

Purl the next 2 rounds to create the seam where the bobby sock folds over. For the next 13 rounds work a simple knit 2, purl 2 rib, which will not show in the fold-over sock but creates a nice fit around the ankle. Next, work the first 6 rounds of the simple eyelet spiral, however, first turn the work inside out. The wrong side of the cuff fabric will be facing out. The live yarn will be on the left-hand needle (Needle 3) instead of the right-hand needle. From this point on, the wrong side of the fabric becomes the right side of the fabric. Needle 3 becomes the new Needle 1, Needle 2 remains the same, and Needle 1 becomes the new Needle 3. A small hole will form due to the change in knitting direction, but it will be nearly imperceptible and can also be repaired with a darning needle. After 6 rounds of eyelets, jump ahead to the heel flap directions.

For the boy's version, begin here! Cast on 40 stitches. Purl the next 2 rounds, then work a simple knit 2, purl 2 rib for 13 rounds. Work 6 rounds of stockinette stitch, then move on to the heel flap.

Knit the Heel Flap

For the heel flap, place the 20 stitches from Needle 2 on a holder for later. Knit across Needle 1 with Needle 3 so that all 20 heel stitches are on 1 needle—these will be your working stitches, which you will now work in rows instead of rounds. Work 19 rows of heel flap in stockinette stitch, always slipping the first stitch to create our selvage. We created a simple reinforced rib by slipping all odd stitches purl side and knitting even. In other words, on your purl rows you should slip 1, purl 1 and on your knit rows work even. You should end with a purl row.

The Sock Knitting Kit

ᘒᕵ Turn the Heel ᕸᘓ

Still working with your 20 stitches, do the following:

* **row 1:** Knit 12 stitches, slip slip knit, knit 1, turn.

* **row 2:** Slip 1, purl 5, purl 2 together, purl 1, turn.

* **row 3:** Slip 1, knit to 1 stitch before the gap from the prior row, slip slip knit, knit 1, turn.

* **row 4:** Slip 1, purl to 1 stitch before the gap from the prior row, purl 2 together, purl 1, turn.

Continue repeating rows 3 and 4 until only 12 stitches remain. On your last set of rows, you will have to skip the last knit 1 or purl 1 since no more stitches will be left.

ᘒᕵ Form the Gussets ᕸᘓ

To make the gusset, we will begin to work in the round again. In order to make your sock have that L-shape from ankle to foot, you will need to pick up stitches on the selvages, and work the instep stitches on the holders back into the round. When you pick up stitches along the selvage, feel free to use your preferred method. We chose to pick up through both halves of the edge stitch, and to loop through from the right side to the wrong side, leaving a raised edge to decorate the outside of the sock. To do this, work as follows:

* **needle 1:** Knit across all 12 heel stitches, then pick up 11 stitches along selvage.

* **needle 2:** Work across the 20 stitches on the holder, from round 7 of the simple eyelet spiral.

* **needle 3:** Pick up 11 stitches along selvage and knit 6 from Needle 1 to split the heel in half again.

You should now have 54 stitches total as follows: 17 stitches on Needle 1, 20 stitches on Needle 2, and 17 stitches on Needle 3.

It is now time to decrease along Needles 1 and 3, in order to get your sock width back to the original 40 stitches. To do this, work decrease rounds every other round as follows:

On Needle 1, knit to the last 3 stitches, knit 2 together, knit 1. On Needle 2, knit across while maintaining the simple eyelet spiral pattern (or just knit across for the boy's version). To maintain the eyelet pattern after round 12, simply begin with round 1 again. On Needle 3, knit 1, slip slip knit, knit to the end. Remember to work a round without decreases in between. Repeat this pattern until only 10 stitches remain on each needle.

〜 Knit the Instep 〜

Knit even until the sock measures 4 inches from the back of the heel, or is the desired length to the base of the toes (in our case, 22 more rounds). Remember to continue the simple eyelet pattern by repeating rounds 1–12 on Needle 2 of the girl's sock.

Shape the Toe

The toe is worked entirely in stockinette stitch. To begin basic toe shaping, you will decrease 4 stitches every other round on 3 needles as follows:

* **needle 1**: Knit to 3 stitches from the end, knit 2 together, knit 1.

* **needle 2**: Knit 1, slip slip knit, knit to last 3 stitches, knit 2 together, knit 1.

* **needle 3**: Knit 1, slip slip knit, knit to end.

Once you have a total of 20 stitches remaining (5 stitches on Needles 1 and 3, 10 stitches on Needle 2), work the above decreases every round until only 2 stitches remain on each needle. Combine the remaining 8 stitches on to 2 needles by combining the stitches on Needles 1 and 4 on 1 needle. Create your seam using the Kitchener stitch, or the three-needle bind off. Finally, turn the sock inside out and weave in all of the loose threads.

Knee-Highs

Stripes & Anchor Socks

You can't go wrong with a cute pair of knee-high socks. Worn with high-top sneakers or high heels, these nautically themed socks are sure to turn heads. Feel free to change the colors, or customize them with your own duplicate stitch design.

Knee-high socks are just that: socks that reach your knee. They are a basic sock shape, but with a much longer leg. When figuring out sizing, measure the circumference of your calf, and then subtract 10 to 20 percent to allow for stretch. These socks should fit snugly, and our version is ideal for a basic ladies' medium/large. You can subtract or add a few stitches from our pattern to make the fit tighter or looser.

Please note that in circular knitting, you may experience a color jog where you've added a new color. To prevent this, knit 1 full round in the new color. Then on the next round, lift the right side of the stitch below (this will be the old color) onto your left needle and knit it together with the first stitch of the new color.

To accommodate the calf's tapered shape, you'll decrease 2 stitches every 4 rounds over the 28 rounds (starting after you've knit the ribbed top), until you have 36 stitches (9 stitches on each needle). We slip slip knit the first 2 stitches of Needle 1 and knit together the last 2 stitches of Needle 4 every 4 rounds to keep our decreases at the back of the leg. Feel free to make your decreases where you like.

Materials

* 5 double-pointed needles (size 7, or size required to obtain correct gauge)
* Stitch marker
* Stitch holder
* Darning needle
* 2 skeins light blue worsted-weight extra-fine merino yarn (we used 208 yards of Karabella Yarns, Aurora 8, #41, for the pair)
* 1 skein dark blue worsted-weight extra-fine merino yarn (we used 76 yards of Karabella Yarns, Aurora 8, #23, for the pair)
* 1 skein cream worsted-weight extra-fine merino yarn (we used 87 yards of Karabella Yarns, Aurora 8, #1350, for the pair)

Gauge (in stockinette stitch)

* 4.5 stitches per inch

Finished Size

* ladies' medium/large

Skills & Methods

* Stockinette stitch
* Duplicate stitch
* Kitchener stitch

⌒ Cast On & Knit the Leg ⌒

Using the double cast-on method, cast on 52 stitches with light blue yarn onto 1 needle. Next, divide the stitches evenly onto 4 needles, 13 stitches on each needle. Join the round, being careful not to twist the stitches. Place a stitch marker at the beginning of the round between Needles 1 and 4.

To create the ribbed top, knit 2 stitches then purl 2 stitches for 4 rounds.

Switch to the cream yarn and work 4 rounds in stockinette stitch, remembering to decrease 2 stitches on round 4.

Switch back to the light blue yarn and work 4 rounds in stockinette stitch, decreasing 2 stitches on round 8.

Switch back to the cream yarn and work 4 rounds in stockinette stitch, decreasing 2 stitches on round 12.

Switch to the dark blue yarn and work 26 rounds in stockinette stitch, remembering to decrease 2 stitches on rounds 16, 20, 24, 28, and 32. You should have 5 stitches each on Needles 1 and 4, and 13 stitches each on Needles 2 and 3. Redistribute the stitches by moving 4 stitches from Needle 2 to Needle 1, and 4 stitches from Needle 3 to Needle 4. Each needle now has 9 stitches. Continue working in stockinette stitch.

On row 39, switch back to cream and work 4 rounds in stockinette stitch.

On row 43, switch to the light blue yarn and work 4 rounds in stockinette stitch.

On row 47, switch back to the cream yarn and work 4 rounds in stockinette stitch.

On row 51, switch back to the light blue and work the next 50 rounds in stockinette stitch. This will give you a leg length of approximately 16 inches.

⤙ Knit the Heel Flap ⤚

To knit the heel flap, knit 9 stitches to the end of Needle 1. Transfer the 18 stitches from Needles 2 and 3 onto a stitch holder for later use. These will be for the instep. Transfer your 9 stitches from Needle 4 onto the end of Needle 1. You will stop knitting rounds while you work on the heel flap, which is created from the 18 stitches now on Needle 1. Turn your work, slip 1 and purl back 17 stitches on Needle 1. To make a slightly sturdier fabric we recommend knitting the heel flap in heel stitch, which is done by slipping every other stitch on each purl row. Work 18 rows in heel stitch, making sure you slip the first stitch of each knit and purl row. This will create a selvage seam of 11 stitches on each side of the heel flap, which you will pick up when you knit the gusset.

⤙ Turn the Heel ⤚

To create a square heel, still working with your 18 stitches on Needle 1, do the following:

* **row 1:** Knit to 2 beyond center (in other words, 11 stitches), slip slip knit, knit 1, turn.

* **row 2:** Slip 1, purl 5, purl 2 together, purl 1, turn.

* **row 3:** Slip 1, knit to 1 stitch before the gap from the prior row, slip slip knit, knit 1, turn.

* **row 4:** Slip 1, purl to 1 stitch before the gap from the prior row, purl 2 together, purl 1, turn.

Repeat rows 3 and 4 until only 12 stitches remain. On your last set of rows, you will have to skip the last knit 1 or purl 1 since no more stitches will be left.

ꙮ Form the Gussets ꙮ

To shape the sock from the ankle to the foot, you will pick up stitches along the selvages on either side of the heel flap and return to working the stitches currently on the stitch holder in the round. Knit across all 12 stitches on Needle 1. Next, pick up 1 stitch through each slip stitch loop along the edge of the heel flap, 11 stitches total. You should now have 23 stitches on Needle 1. Transfer the 18 stitches from the stitch holder evenly onto Needles 2 and 3 and knit across. With Needle 4, pick up 1 stitch through each selvage on the other side of the heel flap (11 stitches total) and knit the first 6 stitches of Needle 1. You should now have 52 stitches, as follows: 17 stitches each on Needles 1 and 4, and 9 stitches each on Needles 2 and 3.

Next, decrease for the gussets every other round as follows:

* **needle 1:** Knit to last 3 stitches, knit 2 together, knit 1.

* **needles 2 and 3:** Knit across.

* **needle 4:** Knit 1, slip slip knit, knit to end.

Repeat this pattern for approximately 15 rounds, until 36 stitches remain, remembering to work a round without decreases in between each decrease round. Divide the stitches evenly among the 4 needles, 9 stitches per needle.

⤳ Knit the Instep ⤳

Knit even until sock measures 7 inches from back of heel, or is the desired length to the base of the toes (in our case, 28 rounds).

⤳ Shape the Toe ⤳

For an added bit of fun, switch to cream yarn and knit 1 decrease round as follows to begin the basic toe shaping:

- **needle 1:** Knit to 3 stitches from the end, knit 2 together, knit 1.
- **needle 2:** Knit 1, slip slip knit, knit to end.
- **needle 3:** Knit to 3 stitches from the end, knit 2 together, knit 1.
- **needle 4:** Knit 1, slip slip knit, knit to end.

Alternate this decrease round with 1 knit round until 20 stitches remain. On round 5, switch to the dark blue yarn and continue decreasing 4 stitches every other round as instructed above. Once you have a total of 20 stitches remaining (5 stitches on each needle), work the above decreases every round until only 2 stitches remain on each needle. Divide remaining 8 stitches over 2 needles by combining the stitches on Needles 1 and 4, and combining those on Needles 2 and 3. Close the toe using the Kitchener stitch. Finally, turn the sock inside out and weave in all of the loose threads.

⤳ Anchor Design ⤳

Using the duplicate stitch method, also known as Swiss darning, add the anchor design to the outer side of the dark blue area of the sock. The anchor design is 13 stitches at its widest, and 24 stitches tall. On the left sock, the anchor is centered along the stitches of Needles 1 and 2. On the right sock, the anchor is centered along the stitches of Needles 3 and 4. Thread your darning needle with approximately 3 yards of the cream yarn. We suggest working the pattern from the bottom up, following the graph below. Insert your darning needle from the wrong side of the sock through the center of the stitch below the V you intend to duplicate (here, the stitch in row 2, column 9). Then go 1 stitch above the V you intend to duplicate, insert your needle and yarn through both legs of the V from left to right, and pull the yarn through. Finally, insert your needle back through the original point of entry. For the second sock of the pair, remember to place the anchor design on the opposite side so that it is on the sock's outer half.

꒰ Anchor Graph ꒱

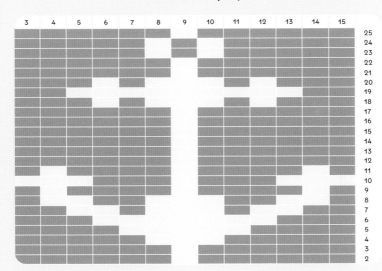

Mukluks

Slipper Socks

We were inspired to knit up a slipper sock that looks like the Sherpa and sheepskin boots that have been so popular recently. This indoor version is just as fashionable, and is a real quick knit when you use super bulky yarn!

This slipper sock is knit from the top down, like most traditional socks, but you will not be knitting the usual rounds until you reach the ankle. From calf to ankle, you will knit what is essentially a shaped flap to accommodate most of the leg circumference. Then you will knit a smaller, rectangular flap—the tongue—for your slipper. When these two sections meet at the ankle, you will proceed with the traditional, basic sock pattern. Because there are so few stitches with this bulky yarn, we used four double pointed needles instead of the usual five. The stitches that were worked on Needles 2 and 3 (the instep) were worked on one needle (Needle 2).

Materials

* 5 double-pointed needles
  (size 13, or size required
  to obtain correct gauge)
* Size I crochet hook
* Stitch marker
* Stitch holder
* Darning needle

* 3 skeins super-bulky wool yarn in
  Linen (we used 180 yards of Rowan
  Big Wool, #16, for the pair)
* 2 skeins brushed alpaca bulky yarn
  in light brown (we used 55 yards
  of Karabella Yarns, Brushed Alpaca,
  #1557 for the pair)
* 1 skein brushed alpaca bulky yarn
  in dark brown (we used 35 yards
  of Karabella Yarns, Brushed Alpaca,
  #1553 for the pair)

Gauge (in stockinette stitch)

* 3 stitches per inch

Finished Size

* ladies' medium

Skills & Methods

* Stockinette stitch
* Seed stitch
* Bobbles
* Kitchener stitch
* Crochet chain

⮌ Cast On & Knit the Leg Flap ⮌

Cast on 28 stitches of the main color, the natural super-bulky yarn. Work in knit 2, purl 2 rib for 2 rows. Continue in stockinette stitch, making 1 increase on the first and last stitch of every other row. You should have 32 stitches on the fifth row. Switch to light brown, brushed alpaca yarn and purl 1 row. Work 9 bobbles (see directions on opposite page) over the next row as follows: knit 3, *make bobble, knit 2, repeat from * 9 times, then knit 2 more to end. (On 1 edge your bobble is set 3 stitches in, on the other edge your bobble is set in 4 stitches.) The bobble is a very simple 3-stitch one, which looks terrific in the brushed alpaca.

To make the bobble, insert your needle as if to knit, pull yarn through without releasing the stitch, yarn over, insert the needle again and pull the yarn through again. You should have made 3 loops from that 1 stitch. Purl back across these 3 loops, then knit across them while decreasing as follows: slip 1, knit 1, pass the slipped stitch over, knit 1 again, and pass the slipped stitch over again. That brings you right back to 1 stitch, and you should have a bobble. You may need to poke the bobble with your finger to get it to look just right.

After the bobble row, switch back to your main color yarn and purl 1 row while working a decrease at the beginning and end of this row so that 30 stitches remain (purl the first 2 stitches together, and purl the last 2 stitches together). Next work 3 rows of seed stitch in the main color. To knit in seed stitch, knit 1, purl 1 on your knit row (the fabric's right side), turn your work, and purl the knits and knit the purls from the previous row. On your third seed stitch row, decrease again by knitting the first 2 stitches and last 2 stitches of the row. You should now have 28 stitches left. Switch to the dark brown alpaca yarn and purl 1 row. Work 8 bobbles over the next row as follows: knit 3, *make bobble, knit 2, repeat from * 8 times, then knit 1 more to end. (On both edges your bobble is set 3 stitches in.)

Switch to your main color and purl 1 row while working a decrease at the beginning and end of this row, so that 26 stitches remain (purl the first 2 stitches together and purl the last 2 stitches together). Next work 3 rows of seed stitch. Switch once again to the light brown alpaca to form the last set of your bobbles. Purl 1 row. Work 8 bobbles over the next row as follows: knit 2, *make bobble, knit 2, repeat from * 8 times. (On both edges your bobble is set 2 stitches in.)

Switch back to the main color. Work 13 rows in stockinette stitch while making decreases at the beginning and end of the knit rows (every other row) by knitting the first 2 stitches together and the last 2 stitches together until only 16 stitches remain. End on a purl row. Put all the stitches on a stitch holder. Before you can begin working in traditional sock rounds, you need to create a tongue flap.

⌒ꞵ Knit the Tongue ꞵ⌒

Using the double cast-on method, cast on 10 stitches in the natural white yarn and work in a seed stitch for 33 rows.

Keep the tongue flap on your needle, and knit 8 stitches off your stitch holder onto a new needle to join your previous work (10 stitches on what will become Needle 2, and now 8 stitches on what will become Needle 3). Using another needle, knit the remaining 8 stitches from the stitch holder on what will become Needle 1. Work 1 round while maintaining the seed stitch pattern on Needle 2, and working decreases on Needles 1 and 3. On Needle 1, knit to last 2 stitches then knit 2 together. On Needle 3, slip slip, knit the first 2 stitches and knit until end. You now have 24 stitches. Work 6 more rounds even in this established pattern so that the seed stitch continues all along the instep (Needle 2) and everywhere else you are maintaining a stockinette stitch (Needles 1 and 3). Finally re-distribute your stitches by taking one stitch from the end of Needle 1 and one stitch from the end of Needle 3 and placing them on Needle 2. You should have 6 stitches on Needle 1, 12 stitches on Needle 2, and 6 stitches on Needle 3.

Now you are ready for the heel flap. Place all of the stitches from Needle 2 on a holder and work in rows again using the combined stitches on Needles 1 and 3 as follows.

∂ꞏ Knit the Heel Flap ꞏ∂

Using Needle 3, knit 6 stitches to the end of Needle 1. Turn the work, then slip 1, purl 1 to the end of the row. Turn again and slip 1, knit across to the end. Repeat this for 11 rows, ending on a knit row, then turn the heel.

∂ꞏ Turn the Heel ꞏ∂

Because there are so few stitches, this is a quick turn!

* **row 1:** Slip 1, purl 7, purl 2 together, purl 1, turn.

* **row 2:** Slip 1, knit 5, slip slip knit, knit 1, turn.

* **row 3:** Slip 1, purl to last 2 stitches, purl 2 together, turn.

* **row 4:** Slip 1, knit to last 2 stitches, slip slip knit.

You have 8 stitches remaining. Time to pick up for the gussets and work in the round again.

∂ꞏ Form the Gussets ꞏ∂

With the needle containing your turned heel stitches (Needle 1), pick up 1 stitch through each slipped stitch loop on the heel flap's selvage. You should pick up 6 stitches and have a total of 14 on this needle. With a second needle (Needle 2) work across stitches on your holder forming the instep, making sure to continue in a seed stitch pattern for the rest of this sock until the toe (total of 12 stitches). With a third needle (Needle 3), pick up 6 stitches along the slipped stitch loop on the other selvage and knit 4 stitches off Needle 1 to center of heel (for a total of 10 stitches). Your stitches are now distributed correctly to begin decreasing: you should have 10 stitches each on Needles 1 and 3, and 12 stitches on Needle 2. Now begin four rounds of decreases on Needles 1 and 3 in order to get back to the desired number of 24 total stitches. Work these decrease rounds every other round while working the seed stitch on Needle 2 only. On Needle 1, knit to last 3 stitches, knit 2 together, knit 1. On Needle 3, knit 1, slip slip knit, knit to end.

❧ Knit the Instep ☙

Once you have reduced your stitches so that there are only 10 each on Needles 1 and 3, continue working even in this established pattern of seed stitch on Needle 2 only, until the slipper measures 6 inches from the heel. In the pictured example, 11 rounds were worked even after the gusset decreases.

❧ Shape the Toe ☙

For toe shaping, standard decreases were worked every other round in stockinette stitch. On Needle 1, knit to the last 3 stitches, knit 2 together, knit 1. On Needle 2, knit 1, slip slip knit, knit to last 3 stitches, knit 2 together, knit 1. On Needle 3, knit 1, slip slip knit, knit to end. When you have only 8 stitches left, combine the stitches on Needles 1 and 3, and fasten off using the Kitchener stitch.

For lacing up the slipper, use the yarn in your main color and a crochet hook to create a chain that is about a yard long. Lace the chain through the loops in the selvage, passing it through every fifth row. On your last lace-up, pull the ends of the crochet chain through the center stitch of the tongue to keep it in place.

Make two 1½-inch pom-poms out of the dark brown fuzzy yarn (see instructions in the Cheerleader Socks pattern) and attach them to your shoelaces.

You may want to purchase adhesive rubber strips from a craft store to make your slippers slip-free!

Pink Stockings

Over-the-knee socks with dark charcoal trim & seed stitch diamonds

Not quite as long as thigh-high stockings, this pair of socks was inspired by vintage lingerie. The colors and luxurious materials of the stockings will make you feel like a pin-up beauty!

Materials

* 5 double-pointed needles
  (size 5, or size required
  to obtain correct gauge)
* Stitch marker
* Stitch holder
* Darning needle

* 3 skeins pale pink DK-weight
  extra-fine merino and cashmere
  blend yarn (we used 334 yards of
  Karabella Yarns, Margrite, #25 for
  the pair)
* 1 skein dark charcoal DK-weight
  extra-fine merino and cashmere
  blend yarn (we used 155 yards
  of Karabella Yarns, Boise, #58 for
  the pair)

Gauge (in stockinette stitch)

* 6 stitches per inch

Finished Size

* ladies' small/medium

Skills & Methods

* Stockinette stitch
* Seed stitch
* Kitchener stitch

Because of the cashmere content of the yarn, these demure stockings feel just as luxurious to knit as they are to wear. They are worked with 4 double-pointed needles throughout the project, with 1 needle used across the back and heel stitches (instead of Needles 1 and 4) to work the pattern of seed stitch diamonds more easily. The heel offers a variation on the traditional gusset, and is knit similarly to a toe decrease. The instructions are sized for a ladies' small/medium. We strongly recommend customizing the fit with a simple measure of the circumference above your knee, and then continuing our basic set of decreases until you reach your desired ankle width. For example, if the circumference approximately 2 inches above your knee is 15 inches, figure out the required amount of stitches based on your gauge for 15 inches, and then subtract 20 percent of the total stitches to account for the stretch of your fabric. From this point, you can follow our basic sets of decreases (maybe a little more, maybe a little less) until you have the amount desired for your ankle. The sock is stretchy and quite forgiving from the ankle down, so it's well worth tailoring the area above the knee.

Cast On & Knit the Leg

Using the double cast-on method, cast on 62 stitches in dark charcoal on 1 needle. Next, divide the stitches onto 3 needles, so that the join falls on the center of Needle 1, with 31 stitches on Needle 1, 15 stitches on Needle 2 and 16 on Needle 3. Work a knit 1, purl 1 rib for 18 rounds. When working knit stitches of a knit 1 purl 1 rib, the needle is usually inserted into the front leg of the stitch to knit. The rib will be more defined if you work into the back leg of your knit stitches instead of the front leg. Switch to pink yarn and work 7 rounds of stockinette stitch.

On the next round, begin the seed stitch diamond by purling the stitch indicated with a dot on the chart on page 56. Center the chart's pattern on Needle 1, with the 16th stitch along the round as the first stitch of the chart. The chart's first stitch will not always be the 16th stitch along, as we will soon commence decreases for calf and ankle shaping, but the chart will always be centered on Needle 1. Work 7 stockinette rounds between the seed stitch diamonds throughout the stocking.

After the second diamond, begin the following sets of decrease rounds. One decrease is worked on alternating needles, as follows, to give a consistent leg shaping. For 20 rounds, every other round works one decrease in alternating locations on the beginning of Needle 1, the end of Needle 1, the beginning of Needle 2, and the end of Needle 3. A total of 10 decreases are made, until 52 stitches remain. In other words:

* **round 1:** Knit the first 2 stitches of Needle 1 together, knit to end.

* **round 2:** Knit even.

* **round 3:** Knit to the last 2 stitches of Needle 1, knit 2 together, knit to end.

* **round 4:** Knit even.

* **round 5:** Knit to the first 2 stitches of Needle 2, knit 2 together, knit to end.

* **round 6:** Knit even.

* **round 7:** Knit to the last 2 stitches of Needle 3, knit 2 together.

* **round 8:** Knit even.

Do this for a total of 10 decreases while maintaining the seed stitch diamond.

After you decrease to 52 stitches, adjust your decreases to every 4 rounds the same way, on alternating needles as above, until a total of 46 stitches remain. (There are a total of 6 decreases, one every 4 rounds). And finally work another set of 6 decreases, this time every 8 rounds, in the same manner until only 40 stitches remain. Work even without decreasing through your seventh diamond and continue to knit 7 more rounds.

ᘒ Knit the Heel ᘓ

We've finally reached the heel. This heel is not a traditional one, and no flap or gussets are created. Instead, knit across the 20 stitches on Needle 1 with a yard of waste yarn in a contrasting color. Then go back to the right side of Needle 1 and knit across the waste yarn with your pink yarn. Work as usual for 8–10 rounds, then place all the stitches on a holder so that you can form the charcoal heel as follows.

Carefully remove the waste yarn while placing the 2 rows of live stitches on 2 needles. You should have a total of 40 live stitches. Pick up an extra stitch on the left side of 1 needle and on the right side of the other needle so you have 21 stitches on each, so that you don't have too big a hole when you start working the heel. Distribute the 42 stitches by transferring 11 to Needle 1, 10 to Needle 2, 11 to Needle 3, and 10 to Needle 4.

Now decrease as you normally do for the sock toe, working decrease rounds every other round as follows. Knit to the last 3 stitches of Needle 1, knit 2 together. Knit, slip slip knit, knit to the end on Needle 2. Knit to the last 3 stitches of Needle 3. Knit, slip slip knit, knit to the end on Needle 4. Do this until only 22 stitches remain.

Combine 11 stitches onto 1 needle and 11 onto a second, so that your 2 needles line up parallel to the width of your foot (and not the length of your leg). Use the Kitchener stitch to fasten these 11 stitches.

ᘒ⸲ Knit the Instep ᘒ⸲

Pick up your pink live stitches again on 3 or 4 needles. In our case we placed all 20 bottom stitches on Needle 1, 10 of the instep stitches on Needle 2, and the last 10 insteps on Needle 3. Work even for about 6 inches.

꩜ Shape the Toe ꩜

Switch to charcoal yarn and begin your standard toe decreases every other round.

* **needle 1:** Knit 1, slip slip knit, knit to 3 stitches from the end, knit 2 together, knit 1.

* **needle 2:** Knit 1, slip slip knit, knit to end.

* **needle 3:** Knit to 3 stitches from the end, knit 2 together, knit 1.

When you only have 8 stitches remaining, divide the stitches between 2 needles and use the Kitchener stitch to fasten off. Weave in all loose ends, and voilà!

꩜ Diamond Graph ꩜

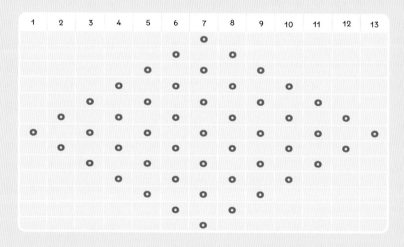

* Glossary *

3-needle Bind Off	A method of binding off two pieces of knitted fabric at the same time in order to create a smooth seam where the two pieces are joined together. It is important to have two needles with the live stitches on them, with an equal number of stitches on each needle. The two pieces should be held together with the right sides of the work facing in (inside out), then a third needle is inserted into the first stitch on each of the held needles, and the two stitches are knit together as one. This is repeated with the next stitch on the two needles until there are two stitches left. With the last two stitches on your third (right-hand needle), pass the first stitch over the second one as you would any time you are binding off. Repeat this pattern of knitting the two next stitches of the original two needles together as one and binding off.
Bobbles	A way of working short rows inside of one stitch and decreasing back to one stitch in certain locations in order to create a decorative raised bump.
Color Jog	When working in the round and switching to different colors, a step or "jog" forms whenever a new color is introduced, usually at the end of the round. Knitted rounds are actually spirals rather than sets of complete circles. Each increasing round therefore is a step up from the previous round. This isn't as noticeable when working rounds in one color.

Decreases	Various methods of reducing the number of stitches in a row or a round. In circular knitting, it is often important to mirror decreases on each side so that they form slants that face each other rather than having the decreases slanting in the same direction. This is done by using knit 2 together on one side, and then slip slip knit (which creates a "mirrored" effect) on the other side, along with several other methods.
Double Cast-on Method	A method of casting on, also called the Continental or Long Tail method. Make a slipknot a few yards from the end of your yarn. Place the slipknot on one needle while the two dangling ends of the yarn are held in the other hand, with the cut end of the yarn looped over the thumb and the attached end of the yarn looped over the index finger. Take the needle up through the thumb loop, over the index finger loop, and down through it, then pull the new loop back through the thumb loop. Drop the loop off the thumb and pull the two strands taut and one stitch has been cast on. Repeat to get the desired number of stitches.
Duplicate Stitch	Using a darning needle and yarn to add contrasting color to an existing item knitted in stockinette stitch. Holding the item with the right side facing you, you will notice a pattern of V shapes created by the stockinette stitch. Focusing only on the Vs, and not the upside-down V pattern, you will also see between the stitch columns. Insert your darning needle from the

Duplicate Stitch (continued)	wrong side at the point just below the V you intend to duplicate. Then insert your needle above either the right or left leg of your V, so that your duplicate yarn is covering that leg. Your needle will be at the back of the work now. Insert the needle horizontally across the back of your work and through to the right side at the point above the other leg. Finally, insert your needle down and through the original point of entry. Your needle will once again be on the wrong side of the fabric, and a duplicate stitch mimicking your knitting will have been completed.
Grafting	A method of connecting two pieces of knitted fabric together without a bulky seam. In particular, the Kitchener stitch used to close the toe in socks.
Gusset	The triangular shape that is created when stitches are picked up along the selvage of a heel flap and subsequently decreased on both sides of that heel.
Instep	The part of the sock that covers the top of your foot. When using 5 double pointed needles, the instep traditionally knits up on Needles 2 and 3.

Intarsia

A method of knitting various blocks of color with separate balls of yarn to follow a pattern of color changes or graph in stockinette stitch. When knitting and purling intarsia, you will drop your old color to the left of the stitch you just worked and bring your new color up into use to the right of the old color. This will twist the new color under the old color just once, interlocking and maintaining an even tension. It's best to practice this a few times with scrap yarn to get the hang of it.

Kitchener Stitch

Using a darning needle and a length of yarn to seam together two pieces of knitted fabric without a bulky seam. There must be an equal number of live stitches on each piece of fabric, then a pattern of weaving yarn as follows is worked through the live stitches to close the seam:

1. Through first stitch on front needle purlwise, through first stitch on back needle knitwise, back through first stitch on front needle knitwise, drop first stitch on front.

2. Through next stitch on front needle purlwise, through first stitch on back needle purlwise, drop first stitch on back needle.

3. Through next stitch on back needle knitwise, through first stitch on front needle knitwise, drop first stitch on front needle.

Kitchener Stitch (continued)	Repeat instructions 2 and 3 until only one stitch remains on each needle, then through last stitch on front needle knitwise and drop, through last stitch on back needle purlwise and drop.
Knit 2 together	A method of decreasing one stitch by knitting two stitches together. This creates a right slant in your knitting.
Rounds, Working In	Creating a knitted tubular finished product using double pointed or circular needles. After casting on the desired number of stitches and being careful not to twist any stitches in the cast-on row, you simply knit the first stitch you cast on to join the round (the needle with the tail end should be your right-hand needle). Each round is knit to create a tube of stockinette stitch. In order to create a tube of garter stitch while knitting in the round, place a marker at the beginning of the row so that you can knit one row and then purl one row, continuing in that pattern.
Rows, Working In	The basic method of creating a flat piece of knitted fabric using two needles and turning at the end of each row of work.
Seed Stitch	A pattern of small bumps created by alternately knitting and purling stitches across rows or rounds. On each subsequent row or round, the stitch that was previously knit is purled and vice versa.

Selvage	The side edge or border of knitting when working rows. In particular, when creating heel flaps, slipping the first stitch of each row can create a cleaner selvage.
Slip Slip, Knit	A method of decreasing one stitch by slipping two stitches from the left-hand needle to the right-hand needle and then knitting them together. This creates a slant to the left, which mirrors the knit two together decrease.
Stockinette Stitch	A basic knitting pattern for creating a smooth knitted fabric. Up close it will resemble a pattern of Vs on the right side of the fabric and a bumpy set of loops on the wrong side. It is created on straight needles by alternating rows of knits and purls. It is created when knitting in the round on circular needles by knitting every row or purling every row.
Ribbing	A combination of knitting and purling in one row, done in a pattern along vertical columns that creates ridges and makes the knitted fabric stretchy. There are infinite patterns of ribs that can be created, but some common ones are two-by-two ribs (which consist of a combination of two knits and two purls) or four-by-four ribs, and so on.
Swiss Darning	Same as Duplicate stitch.

Yarn Over

A method of increasing stitches to make decorative holes in knitting. When knitting, simply pull the yarn in front of the work between the two needle points and loop it over the needle in your right hand before knitting the next stitch. When purling, bring the yarn to the front, and loop it over the right-hand needle and back to the front again before purling the next stitch. On the next row, these loops can be knitted to make a hole and increase the number of stitches, or they can simply be dropped without knitting to create decorative holes without increasing the number of stitches.